Rotational Deaconship
The Bases, History, and Practices

John Olukunle Odejayi

DEDICATION

This masterpiece is dedicated to the ALMIGHTY GOD, the giver of inspiration, knowledge, and grace, for penning this down for the use of His Church.

Second, the book is dedicated to my father, Deacon Daniel Aremu Odejayi, a deacon of excellence, for upholding the faith in the diaconal ministry, despite the challenges he went through with the churches he served.

Third, the book is dedicated to all deacons and deaconesses in Emmanuel Baptist Church, Odo Ona, Ibadan, and the defunct Shalom Baptist Association of the then Oyo West Baptist Conference, for their encouragement and desire to uphold the truth of the word of God.

Fourth, the book is dedicated to all deacons who intend to serve creditably in the diaconal ministry and the pastors who desire to operate a hitch-free diaconal ministry. Shalom!

CONTENTS

v

ACKNOWLEDGMENTS

This work will be incomplete without acknowledging the efforts and contributions of the following people who have worked assiduously to make this research work a point of reference today. First, I cannot forget the efforts of the members of Emmanuel Baptist Church, Odo Ona, Ibadan among whom these teachings were taught, tested, and proved for many years before it turned out to be something worthwhile for the generality of the Church today.

Second, the efforts of the Deacons and Deaconesses of the defunct Shalom Baptist Association and Hephzibah Baptist Association are recognized. These men and women have given me serious platforms for proving these teachings and serving as my experimental grounds. To you all I say, Thank you.

Third, the efforts of Deacon Dr. Gbenga Egbetokun who freely taught me online publishing and encouraged me to make my resources available online for accessibility to the masses and easy publication. May the Lord bless you.

I strongly acknowledge the efforts of my editor, Tolu Falade for her time and contributions to this work. Words of appreciation to colleagues for their encouragement in making this work available. Special appreciation to Revd. Samuel Idowu and all Ministers of the Hephzibah Baptist Association. The effort of Deacon Aderounmu is here put on record for his encouragement so that these resources are available for use.

It will never be out of place to put on record the contributions of my wife (Ruth A. Odejayi) and her encouragement in making this work available. May the Lord bless you all in Jesus' name. Amen.

CHAPTER ONE

What is Rotational Deaconship?

Rotational deaconship can be defined as a method of deaconship whereby someone ordained to serve in the office of a deacon serves for an allotted time after which he/she leaves active service either for some time or indefinitely, to allow someone else to occupy and serve in the same capacity in the church. This period of service which must have earlier been agreed upon by the generality of the church in question before the ordination of the deacons is reflected in the church's constitution with the awareness of all the church members, including each deacon nominated to serve. Therefore, the implication is that every church embarking on this practice must have its modalities spelled out in its constitution which must be made available for every member, including the intending deacons/deaconesses before their selection and approval for service.

Osadolor Imasogie points out that rotational deaconship is a diaconate arrangement whereby a group of deacons serves for a while (and) at the expiration of this period, they are rendered inactive.[1] It implies that *someone or a group of deacons is leaving a stage of Church public active service for others to come in and serve in the same capacity within a specified period. It could therefore be considered a higher calling to serve or a call for renewal of strength for more effectiveness. It would be wrong if it is considered as losing the deaconship status as many people think today since deaconship from inception is not in any way a chieftaincy title. Nevertheless, it should not also be interpreted to mean that one can no longer serve in the house of God or that one becomes redundant as some schools of thought have interpreted it to be. Rather, rotational deaconship draws one out of the church public scene to continue service in obscurity most times while retaining your deaconship status.*

---

[1] O. Imasogie *Deacon in the Local Church.* (Ibadan: Baptist Press (Nig.) Limited, 1996), vii.

CHAPTER TWO

The Biblical Bases and Practice of Rotational Deaconship

A critical look through the Bible reveals that there is no clear-cut passage **directly** referring to rotational deaconship to substantiate its argument or otherwise and although many people have tried as much as possible to link or place it within the context of different passages of the Scriptures, which are inadequate to give a clear and vivid explanation of the concept as people would expect it to be; the question of the need to clarify the biblical bases for this practice lingers on. This is one of the many reasons most church deacons find it so difficult to accept the necessity of the practice in the church seeing it has no clear, vivid, or direct passage of reference in the Bible. This has resulted in the conclusion that it is always the pastor's idea to outwit some deacons in the church especially those who are not in the pastor's good book. This chapter, therefore, aims at clarifying this age-old confusion and seeks to shed more light on the concept to help as many practicing the concept and as many who are confused on its practice, and who want to know its bases from the Scriptures. This chapter first seeks to understand possible *passages quoted by ministers to back up this concept to do justice by way of exegeting the passage(s) and correcting the erroneous interpretation and beliefs if there are any. Also, it should be stated at this point that the bases for the practice of rotational deaconship go beyond the Bible into the history of the church and different responses to issues in the church, which have come to stay today.*

With the above clarifications, it is therefore right to go through the biblical bases for rotational deaconship and this shall be approached as usual. First, from the Old Testament perspective to enable a clearer understanding and justification of its practice and later from the New Testament.

CHAPTER THREE

Traces of Biblical Bases and Practice of Rotational Deaconship in the Old Testament

While a clear-cut declaration of the concept may be difficult to point at in the Scriptures, it will be out of place to say outrightly that rotational deaconship is unbiblical. It would be wrong to say it is unbiblical because taking a good look at what happened in the Old Testament, where the shadow of the practice of deaconship is first discovered (Exodus 18) and some other references to the subject of service in the wilderness Church, one would later discover that God gave a step by step instruction to Moses about the introduction of people into His service to work for Him together with Aaron, and their gradual rotation out of His service at a particular time and age in life.

First, it was the counsel of Jethro to Moses that initiated service among the people of God (Chapter two ref.). Jethro in his counsel never forced Moses to abide by his counsel but admonished him **to yield to whatever God instructed him to do on the same issue** (Exodus 18:23). The implication is that Moses was left to probably seek *the face of God and might have sought the face of God on the matter to know the mind of God before taking a decision. Eventually, as Moses continued in his ministry as the leader of the people of God, there were times when he cried to God for the need for help because the burden was becoming unbearable for him alone (Numbers 11:14-17 ref.).*

Num 11:14 *I am not able to bear all this people alone, because it is too heavy for me.*

Num 11:15 *And if thou deal thus with me, kill me, I pray thee, out of hand, if I have found favour in thy sight; and let me not see my wretchedness.*

Num 11:16 *And the LORD said unto Moses, Gather unto me seventy men <u>of the elders of Israel</u>, whom thou knowest <u>to be the elders</u> of the people <u>and officers over them</u>; and bring them unto the tabernacle of the congregation, that they may stand there with thee.*

Num 11:17 *And I will come down and talk with thee there: and I will take of the spirit upon thee, and will put it upon them; and they shall bear the burden of the people with thee, that thou bear it not thyself alone.*

This was stated clearly when God called Aaron and his sons into the service of God (Numbers 18:1ff), he chose the whole house of Levi as His own and He (Yahweh) as their only portion. It would be remembered that this was done when God chose the Levites for Himself in the place of the firstborn Sons in Israel (Numbers 3:12-13, 40-51, 8:16-18). Therefore, the Levites were replacements for the firstborn sons in Israel and were consequently given to Aaron and his sons as a **gift** for the service of the house of the Lord (Numbers 3:9-12, 8:18-19, 18:6). This was done because the Lord God saw that even though the house of Aaron had been chosen to serve God in the Priesthood office, the work was more than what they could do alone and that they needed helping hands. The Levites (Replica of **Deacons in our context**- Exodus 18:13-26, Acts 6:1-7), therefore, were given to the priest (Replica of **pastors in our context**) to offer helping hands in the ministry, so that the work of the ministry could be easier for them. The implication therefore is that the priests (pastors) are the chiefs of the Levite (Numbers 3:9, 32, 4:19, 28, 33, 1 Chronicles 9:18-20), and every Levite therefore must be submissive to his Priest in receiving instructions from him for daily functions. In like manner, every deacon is required to receive instructions from his/her pastor in the matter of church relations and worship so long he/she accepts him as his/her pastor and agrees to work with him. According to this submission on the Levitical ministries, it could be said that the Levites in their context were the replica of deacons in our context. History has it that during the first six centuries, deacons were referred to as Levites in the church.[2]

Some conditions surround the call of a Levite into the ministry of the Tabernacle. One of such conditions that determines the ordination of a Levite into the Levitical office is the service years (age limit). God himself and not Moses introduced the service year of a Levite (Numbers 4:1-3, 21-23, 29-30, 46-48), starting from the sons of Kohath to the sons of Gershon and the sons of Merari.

Num 4:1 *And the LORD spake unto Moses and Aaron, saying,*

Num 4:2 *Take the sum of the sons of Kohath from among the sons of Levi, after their families, by the house of their fathers,*

Num 4:3 *From thirty years old and upward even until fifty years old, all that enter into the host, to do the work in the tabernacle of the congregation.*

Num 4:21 *And the LORD spake unto Moses, saying,*

Num 4:22 *Take also the sum of the sons of Gershon, throughout the houses of their fathers, by their families;*

Num 4:23 *From thirty years old and upward until fifty years old shalt thou number them; all that enter in to perform the service, to do the work in the tabernacle of the congregation.*

---

[2] S. Cheetham *A History of Christian Church During the First Six Centuries* (London: Macmillan and Co., Limited, 1905), p. 128.

***Num 4:29** As for the sons of Merari, thou shalt number them after their families, by the house of their fathers;*

***Num 4:30** From thirty years old and upward even unto fifty years old shalt thou number them, everyone that entereth into the service, to do the work of the tabernacle of the congregation.*

***Num 4:46** All those that were numbered of the Levites, whom Moses and Aaron and the chief of Israel numbered, after their families, and after the house of their fathers,*

***Num 4:47** From thirty years old and upward even unto fifty years old, everyone that came to do the service of the ministry and the service of the burden in the tabernacle of the congregation,*

***Num 4:48** Even those that were numbered of them were eight thousand and five hundred and fourscore.*

*The implication therefore is that service year is very important for any Levite coming into the service of Yahweh to work alongside the priest. This by application to the church and pastoral ministry implies that the service year should also apply to any deacon coming into the ministry of the church to work alongside any pastor in the church (**Probably to give room for maturity before entering into the service of Yahweh and to ensure*** *effectiveness in the ministry to avoid any possible error because they shall be held responsible and accountable of their service to Yahweh). Note that, as time went by, this age limit was reviewed by God himself, leaving us with the question of the need for review.'*

In the first instance, God instructed Moses that anyone coming into the service of Yahweh as a Levite must have attained a minimum of thirty (30) years of age (Numbers 4:1-3, 21-23, 29-30, 46-48) and must not exceed fifty years of age to remain in the service of Yahweh. The introduction of the service year into the Levitical service was probably to give room for maturity before entering the service of Yahweh and to avoid any possible error because they shall be held accountable for their service to Yahweh during their service year. This also resulted in the need for the introduction of the retirement age, to guide against ineffectiveness which may result from health and other related challenges capable of resulting in counterproductivity which could bring the wrath of God upon His people.

Applying these passages to the contemporary issue, service years are very important in the ministry of deacons in the Church. This is very important first, to give room for maturity (mentally, physically, emotionally, and spiritually) before coming in to serve in this capacity. It is also important to guide against ineffectiveness in the service so as not to bring the wrath of God upon the people of God whom they are called to serve.

In Numbers 8:23-26, God again called Moses to re-emphasize this issue of service year when he was consecrating the Levites to the service of Yahweh and therein pointed out the fact that enlistment for Levitical service should start from age twenty-five (25) and retirement at age fifty (50). Later on in the Chronicles account, David earlier enlisted people for Levitical services at age thirty (1 Chron. 23:1-3) and later on at age twenty and upward when he was handing over the kingdom to Solomon his son (1 Chron. 23:24-28). What could be responsible for these discrepancies? To reconcile these apparent discrepancies, some scholars have suggested that it could probably be for some reasons.

First, it has been suggested that at the time Moses was speaking in Numbers 4:3, the Levitical service was exceedingly severe, laborious and consequently required full-grown, robust men, to perform it. The age of thirty (30) was therefore required as the period of entering into this service. This could further be argued, seeing that God instructed Moses to relieve anyone serving in the Tabernacle from his fiftieth year, probably for health and effectiveness' sake so that his service in the Tabernacle would not incur wrath in the place of blessings upon the people (cf: Numbers 8:18-19). The implication is that, for the laboriousness of the Levitical ministries, strong men are required in this service who can labour without being easily exhausted until the task is fully concluded.

Second, some people have suggested that the twenty-five years of service as raised here implies a five-year probationary period before a Levite fully assumes the service of Yahweh at age thirty. The implication therefore is that a Levite comes to service five years before his actual service year to enable him to learn from other Levites who have gone ahead of him to avoid errors and to be able to master the service well. This has been suggested as the main reason behind the change of service year from thirty years of Numbers 4:3 to the twenty-five years of Numbers 8:23-26. It therefore suggests that God himself was looking for young, capable, and dynamic blood in His service, due to the challenges involved in the service hence, the need for adjustment from older age to younger age.

As time went by, there was a need for further re-adjustment of the service enlistment age. The first thing to note is that during the early years of David's reign, he enlisted the Levites to the service of Yahweh at age thirty (1 Chron. 23:1-3). Whereas in his old age, and especially when he knew that the tabernacle and temple would be fixed and that the laboriousness of the service in the tabernacle would be drastically reduced or no longer be in place, he recommended twenty (20) years as the new enlistment age into the service of Yahweh (Num. 4:3, 4:23, 1Chr. 23:24-32). This according to David was because at the time of this further review of service age, the tabernacle would have been fixed and there would be nothing too backbreaking for the Levites to carry all about. This implies that there will be no need for older and hefty men to bear the heavy loads of the tabernacle but such that will be able to wait on Aaron and his children (the Priests) in the tabernacle, who are prompt and effective in service (1Chr. 23:24-26, 27-32). It suggests that the service year was further reduced because of the reduction or removal of the stress involved in the service of the tabernacle.

Having established the fact that God gave the starting point for the Levitical service in the Tabernacle, another thing that must not be shied away from is the fact that the same God gave the retirement age for the Levitical service. In the same passage under consideration and throughout the passages referring to the Levitical service years, God stated clearly that the retirement age should not exceed fifty (50) years (Numbers 4:1-3, 21-23, 29-30, 46-48) despite the adjustment in the year of entry. The discovery made here is that while God gave the first review of their service year (Numbers 8:24-25), He insisted on the fact that the retirement age should remain fifty (50) years, that is, the retirement age was not reviewed (Numbers 4:1-3, 21-23, 29-30, 46-48). It means that God was mindful of both the recruitment and the retirement age, but was more particular and insistent about the retirement age (Numbers 4:1-3, 21-23, 29-30, 46-48, 8:24-25).

Notwithstanding, what becomes of those who have served in and retired from the service of the Tabernacle and are still agile? According to the instruction of God to Moses and Aaron, such who have retired from the service of the Tabernacle could still be useful although they could no longer do (**be held responsible for**) any (**wait upon the**) service in the Tabernacle; they shall minister with their brethren in the tabernacle of the congregation, **to keep the charge** and shall do no service..." (Numbers 8:25-26). The need for adequate interpretation of this passage requires that the same passage should be considered from other translations of the Scriptures for better and clearer understanding, therefore, the passage in other translations reads:

> They may help the other Levites in their duties, but they must no longer be responsible for any work themselves. Remember this when you assign their duties. (Contemporary English Version)

> Men who are at least fifty (50) years old will be on duty to help their brothers, but they will not do the work themselves. That is what you must do for the Levites so that they can do their duty. (Easy to Read Version)

And from the age of fifty years, they shall withdraw from the duty of the service and serve no more. They minister to their brothers in the tent of meeting by keeping guard, but they shall do no service. Thus, shall you do to the Levites in assigning their duties? (English Standard Version)

And at the age of fifty, he shall retire. After that, <u>he may help his fellow Levites in performing their duties in the Tent, but he must not perform any service by himself.</u> This is how you are to regulate the duties of the Levites. (Good News Bible)

But when they are fifty (50) years old, they must retire from active service and not work anymore. They may assist the other Levites in their duties at the tent of the meeting, but they may not do any regular work. This is how you will handle the Levites' duties. (God's Word)

And from a son of fifty years, they shall return from the service of the work, and shall not serve anymore. But he shall serve with his brothers in the tabernacle of the congregation, to keep the charge; only he shall not serve at a service. So, you shall do to the Levites concerning their charge. (Literary

Translation Version)

And from the age of fifty years, they shall stop waiting upon the service and shall serve no more. But they shall minister with their brothers in the tabernacle of the congregation, to keep the charge; only he shall not serve at a service. So, you shall do to the Levites as to their duties. (Modern King James Version)

And they must retire at the age of fifty. After retirement, they may assist their fellow Levites by serving as guards at the Tabernacle, but they may not officiate in the service. This is how you must assign duties to the Levites. (New Living Translation)

At the age of fifty, they must retire from the work. They can assist their brothers in the tasks in the Tent of Meeting, but they are not permitted to do the actual work themselves. These are the ground rules for the work of the Levites. (The Message)

And at the age of fifty years, they shall retire from the warfare of the service and serve no more, but shall help their brethren in the Tent of Meeting [attend to protecting the sacred things from being profaned], but shall do no regular or heavy service. Thus, shall you direct the Levites in regard to their duties. (Amplified)

But after they become fifty years old, they must retire/not do that work anymore. They may help the other descendants of Levi to do their work at the Sacred Tent, but they must not do the work themselves. That is what you must tell them about the work they will do. (Translation for Translators)

Having read the same verses from different translations of the Scripture, it can be concluded that a Levite is required to retire from active tent service at fifty (50) years of age after which he <u>may</u> be helpful in assisting his fellow Levites but not in active service. Active tent service here refers to active service in the sanctuary, which include the service of offering sacrifices on a daily, weekly, monthly, or annual basis <u>but may henceforth assist in other areas of the sanctuary in making sure people who came to the sanctuary for worship abide by the regulations of worship.</u> This by implication is the rotational Levitical service in the Levitical order. If Levitical ministry in the Old Testament was the shadow of the deacon's ministry in the New Testament to the extent that deacons were sometimes in the history of the Church referred to as

Levites, then, the rotational Levitical service could be said to imply rotational deacons' ministry in our context.

A deacon is expected to rotate out of active service at a particular age or after a period of service year as individual Church agrees. However, rotating out of active service does not imply that he cannot still serve in any other capacity of the Church or be useful in other areas of the church apart from active diaconal services. Active service in this context refers to the public services on the podium/pulpit with the pastor, but he/she could still be engaged in other areas (Numbers 8:26), serving other ministers (deacons) in the church to make their work easier for them, either by counseling or encouraging them in the ministry. This allays the fears of most deacons who feel that pastors agitate rotational deaconship to outwit them or hinder them from serving their God. Rotation of a deacon out from active pulpit service in a church simply implies that he cannot serve on the rostrum again as an ordained deacon in active service after his term of service has elapsed according to the duration stipulated by each church in her constitution.

CHAPTER FOUR

Traces of Biblical Bases and Practice of Rotational Deaconship in the New Testament

The argument raised above has seriously established the basis for the practice of rotational deaconship from the Old Testament perspective; nevertheless, there is a need to further support the argument with the New Testament to balance our study on the same concept. Knowing quite well that the concept of deaconship in the New Testament came to the limelight in the book of Acts of Apostles with the first Church in view. The fact that the Bible is silent about the Christian service in the First Church makes it difficult to say categorically like the Old Testament how the practice of deaconship was conducted, whether rotationally or otherwise.

However, the itinerant nature of the ministry of Philip gives a slight suggestion of what could be happening since the growth and persecution of the First Church made most of the ordained deacons and church members to leave the Church to other places for their Christian services (Acts 8:1ff). What was the state of the

Jerusalem Church after the persecution? What was the state of the diaconal ministry in the First Church shortly after the persecution? Were new sets of deacons re-elected in the first Church or deaconship ceased consequent upon the persecution? If new sets were elected, what happened to the first sets of deacons? This suggests that for the church to keep growing, there is a need for the election of other deacons in the church to replace the earlier elected ones who had been scattered as a result of the persecution of the church, although the Bible is silent about it because of the significance of their service in the church.

Second, as time went by, the ministry of Philip was changed from that of full church based to an evangelistic one (an itinerant minister). The implication is that though Philip was still living in Caesarea with his family, his ministry was no longer fully Church based. He moved from place to place preaching the gospel of our Lord and Saviour Jesus Christ (Acts 8:26ff), whereas he was expected to be a table serving deacon in the first Church. How possible was that? Was the Jerusalem Church still in existence despite the persecution (Acts 8: 1-4)? If 'YES' who were those serving in the diaconal capacities after the death of Stephen and the relocation of Philip? Philip had received a ministerial upgrade (double honour – 1 Timothy 3:13) and consequently requires the need for others to take up his office in the Jerusalem Church as a deacon if the church must keep growing and any vacancy would not be created. The death of Stephen and the upgrade of Philip to the position of an Evangelist coupled with the possibility of further increase in the church calls for the election of more deacons to support the ministry of the church.   All these support the fact that Philip sometimes probably left the office of the deacon in the First Church which in our parlance would be referred to as having rotated out of the office although there is no clear-cut standard laid down by the First Church for its operation.

Since there are few references to the diaconal ministry in the New Testament, another passage that could be used as a basis for this practice is 1 Timothy 3:13 where Paul the Apostle said;

For they that **have served** **well as deacons** gain to themselves a good standing, and great boldness in the faith which is in Christ Jesus. (American Standard Version)

For those **who have done good work as Deacons** get for themselves a good position and become free from fear in the faith which is in Christ Jesus. (Bible in Basic English)

For they **that have used the office of a deacon** well

purchase to themselves a good degree, and great boldness in the faith which is in Christ Jesus. (King James Version)

*For they **that <u>have used</u> the office of a deacon** well, purchase to themselves a good degree, and great boldness in the faith, which is in Christ Jesus. (Webster)*

*For they **that <u>have served</u> well as deacons** gain to themselves a good standing, and great boldness in the faith which is in Christ Jesus. (Reversed Version)*

*For those **who <u>have served</u> well as deacons** obtain for themselves a high standing and great confidence in the faith that is in Christ Jesus. (New American Standard Bible)*

*Those who **<u>have served</u> well gain** an excellent standing and great assurance in their faith in Christ Jesus. (New International Version)*

*With these careful readings from various translations, it is expedient to say that the Greek verb translated "they that have used the office of a deacon" is the Greek word **'diakonesantes'** which is a verb in its aorist tense. An Aorist is a verb tense used to express a past* action in an unqualified way, without specifying whether that action was repeated, continuing, or completed or how long it lasted. In aorist, the action of the verb is thought of as simply happening, without any regard to its continuance or frequency. The implication in this passage is that the servants (deacons) under consideration in this passage did the work well when they were in office which resulted in being considered for a higher and better office. This could either imply that such a deacon was no longer serving in that capacity or may still be there. The issue here is that aorist verbs do not really specify the momentariness or the continuance of the action specified.

Adam Clarke, in his commentary on the passage, said the passage implies that they who, having been tried or proved according to 1 Tim. 3:10 and have shown by their steadiness, activity, and zeal, that they might be raised to a higher office, are here said to have purchased to themselves a good degree, (βαϑμον καλον·) for, instead of having to administer to the bodies and bodily wants of the poor, the faithful deacons were raised to minister in holy things; and, instead of ministering the bread that perishes, they were raised to the presbyterate or episcopate, to minister the bread of life to immortal souls. The implication is that deaconship is not for life but a stepping stone to a higher calling, depending on the level of faithfulness in the practice of the calling. This could be seen in the ministry of Philip who for his faithfulness in the *office was taken unto a higher calling as an Evangelist in the first Church. Becoming an Evangelist in the first Church took him from being a helper (deacon) in the church ministry to becoming one of the fivefold ministers of the church; an Evangelist (cf: Ephesians 4:11-12).*

This argument therefore establishes the fact that the God of the calling expects anyone who serves as a helper (Levites - deacon) in the Church to step out of the call with time to a higher calling, which implies rotating out of the calling into another higher ministry, depending on his/her level of faithfulness. The conclusion therefore is that while the Old Testament expects a Levite to leave the office due to age, the New Testament gives an opportunity of a higher calling to the faithful ones, evidence of which is all around us today in our society and our various churches, as many deacons were seen translating from deaconship to the pastorate, if God sees his/ her faithfulness and choose to call him/her to the higher calling. Faithful deacons would be seen to grow in their relationship with God which most times eventually result in the discovery of personal ministries. This is a higher call that hereafter may take him out of a deacon's ministry of a local church as it happened to Philip, the Evangelist.

CHAPTER FIVE

Rotational Deaconship in Church History

If the practice of rotational deaconship could be traced to some meaningful extent in the Bible (Old and New Testaments), the question of whether it was practiced at any time in the history of the church is pertinent. This section seeks to trace the practice of this concept in the history of the church to affirm the authenticity of its validity and seek to know the possible challenges encountered in its operations in the past, how it was handled, and whether the same proffered solutions could be applied to challenges confronting its operations today in local churches.

Since much could not be said about rotational deaconship in church history, it is possible to conclude that something similar to that was in place in the history of the Church. This was in line with the argument of *John E. Burkhart* who notes that, occasionally deacons were elected to become bishops.[3] Does this imply changing their office after a while for something else? A clear example of this is referenced by Merrill C. Tenney in his

---

[3] J. E. Burkhart 'Deacon' *A New Dictionary of Christian Theology.* Alan Richardson & John Bowden (Eds.) (London: SCM Press Ltd., 1983), p. 144.

book 'New Testament Times' where he notes that Ignatius, who later became the Bishop of Antioch early in the second century had once been a deacon of Antioch.[4] The implication is that he had once served in the diaconal capacity before he was considered fit for the office of a Bishop in Antioch. Does this not imply the interim nature of that office? This understanding reveals that the practice of leadership in the history of the church was successive and hierarchical. But, due to certain restrictions placed upon the growing extent of the diaconal functions as early as the Council of Nicaea in AD 325, the nature of the diaconal ministry in the Western churches gradually became subordinate, temporary, and ceremonial, although it retains its original nature in the Eastern churches during the Middle Ages.[5] It would not be out of place to note that the rotation of deacons in the Southern Baptist began in the nineteenth century.[6]

---

[4] M. C. Tenney, *New Testament Times* (London: Inter – Varsity Fellowship, 1965), p. 318.

[5] J. E. Burkhart 'Deacon' *A New Dictionary of Christian Theology.* Alan Richardson & John Bowden (Eds.) (London: SCM Press Ltd., 1983), p. 144.

[6] Roley C. Bailey, *Training for Servanthood, A Basic Training Guide for Baptist Deacons'* Accessed from www.vbmb-wpengine.netdna-ssl.com on 14th June 2019.

The 'Operations' of Rotational Deaconship:

With the aforementioned at heart, it becomes pertinent to discuss the 'how' of the operations of rotational deaconship in a local church, especially in a local assembly where the lifetime active deaconship has been in operation for ages. It would be noted that in the majority of churches where the Pastor works at shifting from the old style of deaconship to the new practice, a serious sense of rancour results between the pastorate and the diaconate. The question is: why?

Sincere consideration of the possible reasons behind this has shown that most times it is because the church is ignorant of the concept and in such a situation needs to be taught carefully and patiently. This implies that no pastor should be in a haste to operate this system of deaconship once his church has not gained the required understanding of this method of diaconal ministry and are ready to operate it. Research has also shown that most churches resist it because the manner of approach of the system shows that the pastors are biased and as a result have some things at heart when introducing the concept, *hence, the church is ready to fight the pastor and resist the idea tooth and nail.*

Does the fact that a deacon rotates out of an active pulpit ministry mean that he can no longer serve as a deacon in the church? Does it imply that he is relegated from his office as a deacon? Does it imply that someone else has taken his position and as a result could not serve in the capacity of a helper in the church? These and many more need careful biblical responses and shall be given closer consideration in this section.

Biblically, a Levite that rotates out of office after fifty years of age continues to serve the Lord but with restraint. His service after fifty years is according to the request of his fellows for his service (Numbers 8:23-26). By implication, once a Levite is up to fifty years of age and still agile to serve, though he is no longer in active service, he could still be used once in a while as the priest deems fit. One serious factor that is responsible for rancour in most churches today is a situation where deacons who have rotated out of service are required to sit down never to be consulted or used in the church. Being human, they are bound to feel relegated and unrecognized and consequently react. That is not the whole Scripture on this matter. How healthy should rotational deaconship be practiced in a local assembly?

The right practice of rotational deaconship requires that the church be rightly taught the essentials of this style of deaconship since it is new to the previous practice the church is used to. Apart from emphasizing the need for the church to embrace its operations, it is important to teach the church and the deacons concerned about their fate after rotating out of office. This is very important because it will allay the fear of those deacons and prepare them to face another phase in life. First, it should be reiterated here that the Levites that rotate out of office at age fifty could be used for some assignment in the Tabernacle at the discretion of the Priest (Numbers 8:25-26). This statement is not of compulsion but of probability when their service is thought of as being needed. However, the service of a deacon who might have served well will surely be needed, but that decision should be left for the Pastor to make at the time. While his service may not necessarily be needed for active pulpit ministry, his service could be needed for extra Church activities as it applies to each assembly. The pastor will have to take this decision and assign such deacons for services in the church. This enables them to keep pace and be engaged in effective Christian service in the church. The summary is that the fact that a deacon rotates out of active pulpit service does not imply that he is no longer serviceable. The implication is that he rotates out of active pulpit service to other forms of services, either in or outside the church which may be either church-based or personal ministry-oriented as God gives him insight. If the church and *deacons have this understanding before engaging them for service or during service, it will rightly prepare them to use their service year well and prepare adequately for their moment of rotating out of effective pulpit service. This will also prepare them to seek the mind of God for what He would want them to engage in by way of Christian ministry after the church service years.*

In conclusion, regarding all the arguments and facts raised on rotational deaconship, the question is whether the practice has any merit or demerits for which it should either be embraced or rejected. Critical analysis of the concept and its practices has shown that rotational deaconship is good, and healthy for the growth of a local assembly and should be embraced because it has some helpful advantages for the growth of the church, despite its possible disadvantages, which was the main reason the diaconal ministry was first considered and approved by the Apostles in the first Church (Acts 6:1-7). However, it would as well be unjustified to say it does not have its demerits, although the merits could be said to outweigh the demerits. It is on this note that both its merits and demerits shall be considered with preference given first to its merits and later to its demerits.

CHAPTER SEVEN

Merits of Rotational Deaconship

Irrespective of the historical and biblical bases and the biases for/against the practice of rotational deaconship, one thing is sure and that is the fact that rotational deaconship has its merits and demerits, wherever it is practiced. Booker T. Washington, a United States educator and political activist once said, 'his experience is that there is something in human nature which always makes an individual recognize and reward merit, no matter under what color of skin merit is found.'[7] What therefore are the advantages of rotational deaconship to a church that desires to grow and keep growing?

Part of the merits of rotational deaconship are: it aids spiritual maturity and allows service to go around, it controls the monopoly of leadership, creates room for effectiveness, aids renewal of strength, and grants long life for more effectiveness to deacons who have served. Other advantages of rotational deaconship are:

1. It grows a church.

---

[7] Booker T. Washington Brilliant Quote

2. It contributes towards the spiritual impact of a church in her locality.
3. It checks leadership monopoly.
4. It aids spiritual maturity and allows service to go around in the church.
5. It strengthens the leadership of the church for more effectiveness.
6. It strengthens and enlarges the ministries of the church.
7. It affords renewal of strength for serving deacons.
8. It affords new and effective men the opportunity of service in the body of Christ.
9. It brings about consistency in church growth.
10. It makes a church consistent and effective in evangelism & outreaches.
11. It creates room for productivity and not just office occupancy.
12. It helps guard against irredeemable errors in the church ministries.

Each of these merits shall be given a close consideration one after the other to enhance better understanding.

1. It Grows a Church

The desire of God for His church is to keep seeing her growing in leaps and bounds. The call placed on the church by her Lord is not only to increase numerically but *spiritually, and one such way to increase spiritually is for a church to embark on rotational deaconship. How does operating rotational deaconship aid the spiritual growth of a local church?*

One important truth every church must be reminded of at this juncture is that, while every church worker is a potential deacon (helper, servant), every church worker is not an ordained deacon. The implication is that every growing church member has the potential of serving in the capacity of an ordained deacon if he/she is rightly selected to serve, and when this is made known to the church, it makes the church keep growing its members regularly so that it is not the serving few that keep serving and keep growing.

Adequate understanding of service will make every member know that he/she has a contribution to make towards the growth of the church and this understanding makes it compulsory for the church to continue to build its membership strength instead of simply accumulating members for financial and numerical growth. Knowing that some people will rotate out of their office and be replaced with time, opens the eyes of the church leadership towards preparing other people for leadership who would take over from them. Therefore, investing in men by building the church's spiritual strength becomes the only option in sustaining this practice of rotation of deacons in the church leadership, if the church must maintain capable hands in their service to the LORD. Therefore, rotational deaconship results in church growth when taken up with this mind and followed up accordingly.

2. It Contributes to the Spiritual Impact of a Church in her Locality.

The moment the first set of deacons were elected, the work of God increased in the church and all around the church. This is one way the community feels the impact of the church around her. As deacons continue to labour, they gradually become weaker due to various challenges all around them. The gravity of their impact is felt reduced in their locality. To keep the pace growing, there is a need to keep changing the baton regularly for the good work to continue and the positive impact of the church to be felt around her emplacement.

This is very important because the moment the impact of the church is no longer felt as before, there is all possibility for earlier efforts to be forgotten and the church may eventually go into a spiritual extinction. Rotational deaconship renews the strength of the serving deacons and thereby makes the work of the church effective within her neighbourhood.

3. *It Checks Leadership Monopoly*

In the majority of leadership scenes, monopoly of leadership is one vice difficult to check, except something has been put in place before the leader comes in place. In fact, in some situations where a check has been put in place, men sometimes look out for whatever could be done to counter whatever has been put in place. Some people struggle hard to extend their stay in office as may be seen in the political scene of some countries in Africa. While this has been said to be common among Blacks, it should here be reiterated that it is not in any way the issue of complexion but that of human nature. It is human to want to remain in office and be 'in charge' as long as the benefit of office remains.

One tectonic advantage of rotational deaconship is that it puts a check on the monopoly of leadership. An important truth that the church must not shut its eyes against is that some of the people coming into the leadership positions in some of our churches today, including the diaconal ministry, are not saved and as a result, they see service as a position of authority and means of exercising power and influence. This has so much affected leadership to the extent that people chosen to be in place of leadership do not in any way consider it as service both to God and humanity and consequently losing out in the area of fulfilling what is expected of them. To such people who never understand that leadership is all about service, rotational deaconship helps to break their monopoly and bring other people who understand what leadership is all about and who could use their God-given office well to achieve the purpose of the kingdom of God.

4. It Aids Spiritual Maturity and Allows Service to go Around.

Another advantage rotational deaconship affords the church is that it allows the opportunity for services in the body of Christ to go around. By implication, it helps the church invest so much in developing its members to maturity to gain people who could serve the body of Christ effectively. A church that does not develop its membership strength to maturity will keep having its services being undertaken by the same set of people while some others will be unavailable for service due to spiritual immaturity. This in turn will hinder the spread of the church's work as only a few will have the privilege of service in the household of faith.

The challenges of spreading and possessing more ground for the Lord require that more hands be available for the work of God; that in turn requires that more people are raised to serve in the church within the scope of their God-given capability. Rotational deaconship therefore allows some other people to come up with new *and fresh ideas to serve where some other people have served and possibly failed or with lesser yield to bring in their possible contribution(s) into the service of God for greater yield. It motivates the congregation to see more leaders developed who can take the place of those who rotate out.[8] The consequence is that it turns out to encourage mutual efforts at building upon the foundation laid by others who have gone ahead.*

5. It Strengthens the Leadership of the Church for more Effectiveness

If the church's work will be more effective, there is a need for the church to learn to embark on rotational deaconship. According to Acts 6:7, the selection of the first set of deacons brought about growth in the church's work and expansion of the ministry. This was because a new set of people with spiritual strength were brought into the ministry. However, noteworthy is the fact that as they continue in the ministry, they will gradually be ineffective due to natural factors like age, abated strength, and many more challenges coming their way, which cannot be denied. This is also a responsible factor for the majority of people serving in leadership positions of which deacon's ministry is not excluded. A sometimes-effective deacon

---

[8] M. Dever and P. Alexander *The Deliberate Church: Building your Ministry on the Gospel* (Wheaton: Crossway, 2005), p. 160.

gradually turns weaker as time goes by, resulting in his/her ineffectiveness in the church's work.

To create room for effectiveness in the church's work, there is a need to allow deacons to rotate out after some years of service to renew their strength, regain new strength, and become more effective for future services in the vineyard of God.

6. It Strengthens and Enlarges the Ministries of the Church

Another advantage of rotational deaconship is that it strengthens and enlarges the ministries of the church. How does it strengthen and enlarge the ministries of the church? On the first hand, it should be noted that rotating out of a particular area of service for someone else to come in on a good note affords the one rotating out to know that he is not permanent in that office but that he/she has a brief time of service. This therefore makes him/her conscious of the need for accountability of whatever he is doing at any time. It further encourages him/her to rightly pursue his/her dreams with utmost care and vigour within the space of time allotted to him/her. Consequently, it makes it possible for anyone who takes over from him to pursue the dream with lesser difficulty. The implication is that building upon the vision of the first set of deacons in particular will be easier thereby strengthening the vision of the church.

Since no deacon is expected to be idle after rotating out of active service, God expects such deacons to be up and doing for God. Therefore, what would they be doing? The Bible emphasizes the need for such deacons to help their brethren in the sanctuary (Numbers 8:26-NIV). This, in our days, implies that a deacon who has rotated out of service can serve in other arm(s) of the church which could be other ministries of the church or a specialized ministry outside the church setting for the glory of God and the growth of His kingdom. The implication therefore is that when a deacon serves well in his office, he indirectly wins the approval of God for a higher calling, thereby enlarging the ministries of the church.

7. It Affords Renewal of Strength for Serving Deacons

One other benefit of rotational deaconship is that it allows the serving deacon(s) to renew their strength to be more effective in God's service. One truth that must not be overlooked is the fact that in every service, anointing and grace are expended and as a result, the need for renewal of strength is inevitable and of paramount importance. Jesus Christ revealed this in his encounter with the woman with the issue of blood who touched him in faith and virtue went out of Him to cause healing (Mk. 5:25-30). By implication, every ministration or service rendered is an indication of expended grace that requires renewal, if the minister would last in the ministry. Jesus requires that His disciples come to the wilderness to rest and renew their strength.

In the perspective of the prophet Isaiah, it is only those who wait upon the Lord that will renew their strength (Isaiah 40:28-30). The importance of renewal of strength for effectiveness and relevance in the ministry requires that like ministers have their annual leave periods and retreats, deacons should be allowed to retreat to be more effective in the ministry and one of the ways such could be done is to practice rotational deaconship.

George Dye, a former South Carolina Baptist Convention President said that having gone around churches, he discovered that one major reason he would recommend rotational deaconship is because faithful deacons in the ministry of the church have burned out because of health reasons and have not been able to carry out their duties.[9] To afford deacons the opportunity to renew their strength, rotational deaconship should be practiced regularly by the church.

---

[9] G. Dye 'Deacon Rotation is Good Idea.' Retrieved on June 30th, 2016 from www.baptistcourier .com/at about 14:31pm.

8. It Affords New and Effective Men Opportunities for Service.

One other thing needed for the church to maintain its growth regularly is to have effective men and women in the service of God. This can be made possible as older serving men who have served at one time or the other leave the stage for younger and agile men to continue the service and help build on the foundation they have laid. As the older men leave the stage of service, potent and agile men are brought into the service, however, there is a warning here for the church and especially for those involved in the nomination and screening of whosoever is coming to serve in this office: be sure right men and women are shortlisted for the office. There is a need for this warning because their nomination and screening process will determine who comes to serve in that capacity for another period which is bound to make or mar the ministry of the church.

It is unfortunate today that the majority of the problems caused in the church, especially from the diaconal ministry are because some people were either nominated to serve in this capacity or not nominated. By implication, some in an attempt to fault the whole nomination exercise nominate their candidate and vote him in so that their interest and not the interest of the church prevails, thereby causing the work of the kingdom of God to drag slowly.

Once the newly nominated men and women for these offices are effective as the earlier ones, then the kingdom's vision continues and grows on daily basis. A careful look into the church reveals that there are such men in our churches; men of new vigour and vision, men who could go extra miles for the kingdom of God. Such men should be brought into the service of the Lord while they are still agile and capable of serving and the exhausted ones should be allowed to rest while performing some lesser functions in the Church behind the scene.

9. It Brings about Consistency in Church Growth

The result of the ministry of the first set of deacons in the first church was that the church grew and many were added to faith, which in the twenty-first-century church language will be termed 'church growth.' This implies that adequate diaconal ministry in the church results in church growth. How can the church keep growing and never lose its taste and strength with time? In this line, one major challenge facing the church is that, while the church desires to keep growing, most of the people who would work with her in actualizing her dreams are getting older and weaker. It is on this note that the church needs to consider what to do to be consistent in her growth. To do this, there is a need to retain capable *hands in the ministry of deaconship which will require that rotational deaconship must be embraced as the option.*

If deacons serve for a while and leave the stage for other capable hands to serve, it will turn out to mean that the good work started will continue without any form of hindrance or delay. It implies that men of equal vision coming to take over the baton will be able to rigorously pursue the goal and work assiduously at achieving the common goal. It further suggests that; men of vision will never be hindered by common natural complaints and as a result see their visions wasting away because of their inabilities. On this note, rotational deaconship should be duly considered as the only option to be embraced in all churches and well spelled out in individual church constitutions.

10. *It Challenges the Church to be Consistent and Effective in Soul-Winning.*

One of the reasons why the good works sometimes started by some of our churches in the area of soul-winning do not continue is because the then agile deacons who had the vision are already cheated by age, sickness, or any other disabilities, which could not allow them to be effective or carry on the good work even when they want to continue and the church does not have somebody else to serve in that capacity. A painful reality is the fact that no matter how useful someone is, one day he will have to leave the stage of activity to the audience. To make the church consistent in her dreams and vision, there is a need for other men to carry on the vision. This therefore is one of the merits of rotational deaconship.

The meaning of this to serving deacons is that being in the office implies that they too should be working hard at developing people to spiritual maturity. When spiritual maturity is of utmost importance to every serving deacon and the Church Pastor, then the Church will never lack in having someone to take over from the other in Christian service. This makes rotational deaconship an easier task to operate anywhere with values.

Rotational deaconship makes the church consistent and effective in the great commission because the enormity of the task requires that capable men be at work. They should be men who could be called upon at anytime, anywhere to go or attend to any assignment on behalf of the church. If such are chosen at any time to the ministry of deaconship, the result is that the church will not slack in her evangelistic vision, and as a result, the church will continue her God-given assignments.

11.   It Creates Room(s) for Productivity over and against Office Occupancy.

Another advantage of rotational deaconship is that it gives room for productivity instead of ordinary office occupancy for the serving deacons in the period of his/her service. One thing that is common to men, especially on this side of the globe (Black Africa) is for men to hold offices for title's sake without contents. Many people want themselves known as Bishops, Reverend Doctors, Pastors, Deacons, etc. even when they offer nothing.

Operating rotational deaconship will help and challenge every potential deacon to know that his/her service is for a short time and as a result to make him/her work hard at making the allotted time meaningful. In making the time meaningful, one thing that results includes productivity and not just office occupancy. When a deacon is very effective and productive while serving, this opens the doors of ministries to him/her before or after leaving the office so that, after completing his service year in the church, he has something to continue with for the Lord. If one serves God well during his/her service years, he/she must have discovered different areas of service for God, which would make leaving the church public office of no offense or regret to him/her because he/she leaves the public scene to continue in a greater ministry committed to him/her by God.

12. It Guides Against Irredeemable Errors in the Church Ministries

A fact that must not be overlooked is that as people serving in the diaconal ministry advance in age, they begin to face some challenges which may include health challenges, failing memories, and lots more, depending on the personality involved and how he has used himself before now. It suggests that they may no longer be capable of doing some things like before and gradually become inaccurate in their thinking or judgments, consequently failing in some responsibilities, which may eventually result in unintentional failures in their ministries and which may be least expected of them. It is on this note that the need for rotational deaconship is clamoured to make the Church work more effectively and flawlessly.

Looking back into the Old Testament, it would be discovered that anyone serving in the ministries of the Temple is expected to carry out his duty with utmost accuracy and without error because he is carrying the offering of God.

> *And the LORD said unto Aaron, Thou and thy sons and thy father's house with thee shall bear the iniquity of the sanctuary: and thou and thy sons with thee shall bear the iniquity of your priesthood (Numbers 18:5).*

This is the reason God made every provision for the Priesthood to avoid distractions that could result in error.

> *And, behold, I have given the children of Levi all the tenth in Israel for an inheritance, for their*

service which they serve, even the service of the tabernacle of the congregation. Neither must the children of Israel henceforth come nigh the tabernacle of the congregation, lest they bear sin, and die (Numbers 18:21-22).

The fact that the Lord God does not allow error in the Tabernacle possibly resulted in God giving room to Levites to rotate out at age fifty because their excuses may not be tenable to God. In the same vein, rotational deaconship helps in guarding against untenable excuses on the altar of God in the ministry. Some older deacons due to age and bad eyesight are no longer accurate in reading the Scriptures. Sometimes, due to age and loss of strength, some deacons take time before they stand and ascend the pulpit. In fact, some could not serve within the space of time allotted to them because they were getting old and could not serve again as before. These and many more call for the need to embrace and embark on rotational deaconship in our various churches.

The above-mentioned are some of the possible merits of operating rotational deaconship in local assemblies. Does that suggest that this operation in a local church is without its challenges? No! Below are some of its demerits which must not be disregarded if it is going to be rightly operated in churches.

CHAPTER EIGHT

Demerits of Rotational Deaconship

Since it is a general belief that whatever has its merit must have its demerits no matter how little, the same principle applies to the practice of rotational deaconship in the local church, especially as it affects the church more than the concerned persons (the deacon). The practice of rotational deaconship is likely to result in a lack of continuity of dreams and vision; where there is no proper handing over (especially where rotational deaconship is not as such embraced), breeds enmity in the church against the pastor or its advocates. It could be used intentionally by some pastors to remove their unwanted serving deacons from the diaconal ministry of the church and many more. This understanding of possible demerits calls for the need for every church intending to go into the practice of rotational deaconship to carefully pray and trust God to help her even as she operates an open policy, depending totally on the Holy Spirit to help her out in her practice of the system in the church so that nothing is carnally influenced. This author, therefore, seeks to take a brief look at each of these possible demerits for the understanding of his readers and as many *in the practice of rotational deaconship.*

1. Lack of Continuity of Dreams and Visions

One of the major demerits of rotational deaconship is that it could result in a lack of continuity of dreams and vision where there is no proper handing over (especially in churches where rotational deaconship is not wholly embraced or wherever a foul play in the selection of another set of deacons is suspected). This is common in most churches whereby one deacon refuses to hand over to another deacon simply because of a particular problem. This could result in the death of a particular vision or dream initiated by the outgoing deacon and as a result, affect the vision of the church. It is on this note that every church intending to embark on rotational deaconship is enjoined to take time in educating every outgoing deacon or those rotating out properly to guide against possible rancour in the church.

Second, churches should insist on electing men and women with genuine salvation experience into the church service. When deacons are dead to the flesh, then they are dead to sin. When they are dead to sin, it will be difficult for them to struggle for position and cause problems for the church of God they are called to serve. Another way the church could guide against this is to turn every vision of a worker, so long it is a viable vision, into the vision of the church. This means that no feasible vision should be allowed to operate at the church level as a personal vision but a corporate vision so that when the visioner is no longer available, the church can go on to operate that vision, with or without him. When a vision is translated from being a personal vision to a corporate one, it eventually outlives the visioner and becomes the organizational vision which could freely be operated by the organization with its terms.

2. Encourages Pastoral Biases.

It is just unfortunate to hear that some of the so-called men of God are no wise men of God. Having established the fact that rotational deaconship has its bases in the Bible, it is important to note that some pastors who operate the concept sometimes have their individual biases due to their experiences and ignorance. This is simply because some of these men of God, possibly because of their denominational policies, have seen some of the so-called deacons as threats to them and their ministries. On this note, everything is done to undo or outsmart some of these deacons. Some pastors have therefore introduced rotational deaconship as one of the possible means of removing unwanted deacons in the church. However, the question is, is their ministry being fulfilled as a result of the removal of these unwanted deacons who have served one way or the other as thorns in the flesh? While this author is not submitting that there is no possibility of some deacons turning out as thorns in the flesh of some pastors, it should be noted that everything works together for the good of those who love the Lord, to those who are the called according to His purpose (Romans 8:28). If a deacon is allowed in your ministry by God, removing him at your will without God will imply that you are undoing yourself, as he/she must have been planted in your life for a purpose. All you need at such a time is to hand it over to God who knows the best approach to remove him or her or handle the situation wholly for your benefit (2 Corinthians 12:7-10).

It has been noted that the majority of pastors who enforce the practice of rotational deaconship do not operate the concept base on the Biblical understanding of the concept but sometimes to satisfy their desires and to bring in whosoever they want into the leadership of the church. Pastors are here encouraged to be careful of their motive when introducing this concept to the church and be careful in teaching the church and be mindful that the church understands the teaching very well to the extent that the idea taught is translated to becoming the idea of the church rather than of the Pastor's before it is eventually implemented in the church. By implication, the practice of rotational deaconship should not be implemented by force but with an understanding of the people.

Rotational deaconship should not be seen or used

as a disciplinary measure or control measure in removing unwanted personnel from among the deacons in the church but instead, trust God as you pray through for their salvation and brokenness. To avoid being termed as biased or being misunderstood when introducing this practice to the church, pastors should have settled the need for the operation of rotational deaconship when the relationship between him and the church deacons is cordial and not when the relationship is out of place. It means that the decision to operate rotation deaconship in any church should never be borne at a time when the church is not at peace.

3. **Breeds Enmity in the Church against the Pastor or its Advocates**.

If any so-called man of God uses this avenue to outwit any deacon in the church, another possible demerit in the operation of the rotational system of deaconship is that it could cause enmity between the church pastor and the affected deacons. This is possible in the situation where some of the affected deacons feel that they are not to rotate out at a point in time. They may feel some people connived together, possibly with or without the knowledge of the pastor, to rotate them out of office.

Rotational deaconship should not be suggested in any church at such a time when the church is passing through leadership challenges but at such a time when the church is at peace so that the good action will not be misinterpreted.

4. *Loss of Some Faithful and Committed Deacons*

In rotational deaconship, one other disadvantage of the practice is that as much as ineffective deacons are rotating out, effective and faithful ones would also be affected with time. At such a time, it seems painful to the pastor or the church. However, if the church has done her work through her Pastor in training more men and the church is firm on its stand never to select men who are not capable of serving into the capacity, it suggests that capable men would always be available in the church and such only would be brought into the ministry of the church.

Second, the church must be consistent in its decision once the operation starts without being mindful of who is affected. The church is not expected to have favourites in leadership when it comes to selecting people to serve else; the health of the church is compromised and breakaway is inevitable. The above-highlighted merits and demerits should be enough to serve as a guide for any church intending to embark on this mode of leadership to take her decision.

Having raised issues on this concept of rotational deaconship which must have opened your eyes towards understanding this concept, it is important to conclude on this note that the practice of rotational deaconship requires an open mind and the leadership of the Spirit. The concept requires openness of the church and her pastor(s) to the Lord and new revelations as it comes their way, and strongly believe such revelation could work, once it has the backing of the Lord. When the church is opened to the Spirit of the Lord, it shall be easier to operate the system without any hitch but with testimonies of His faithfulness.

Another thing needed is a yielded heart to the leadership of the Holy Spirit on a daily basis. The church and its leaders must allow the Spirit of God to keep directing them and inspiring them on what to do. If such is the case, most misunderstandings in churches would have not ensued. Beloved, with all your pursuits, let the Spirit of God be your guide always to provide His leadership in all your ways.

Accurate records should be kept of the rotation of deacons by any church that operates a rotational deaconship system. This is essential so that error is avoided in the operation. Robert Sheffield suggests that the Secretary to the deacons' fellowship be saddled with the responsibility of monitoring the status of each deacon and appreciating them for the service rendered to the church.[10] This will enable the leadership of the church to know when a particular deacon came on board and when

---

[10] Robert Sheffield 'Deacon Rotation' Retrieved on June 30th, 2016 from www.cms.flbaptistonline .net/Deacon Rotation at about 15:23.

he is due to rotate out of service. With all these, the operation of rotational deaconship in churches should be less troublesome, as we allow the leadership of the Spirit in all our operations in the church.

WORKS CITED

Bailey, R. C. *Training for Servanthood, A Basic Training m Guide m for Baptist Deacons'* Accessed from *www.vbmb-wpengine.netdna-ssl.com* on 14th June 2019.

Booker T. Washington Brilliant Quote

Burkhart, J. E. 'Deacon' *A New Dictionary of Christian Theology*. Alan Richardson & John Bowden (Eds.) London: SCM Press Ltd., 1983.

Cheetham, S. *A History of Christian Church During the First Six Centuries* London: Macmillan and Co., Limited, 1905.

Dever, M. and Alexander, P. *The Deliberate Church: Building your Ministry on the Gospel* Wheaton: Crossway, 2005.

Dye, G. 'Deacon Rotation is Good Idea.' Retrieved on June 30th, 2016 from www.baptistcourier .com/at about 14:31 pm.

Imasogie, O. *Deacon in the Local Church. Ibadan: Baptist Press (Nig.) Limited.*

Sheffield, R. 'Deacon Rotation' Retrieved on June 30th, 2016 from www.cms.flbaptistonline.net/Deacon Rotation at about 15:23 pm.

Tenney, M. C. *New Testament Times* London: Inter–VarsityFellowship, 1965.

About the Author

John Olukunle Odejayi is a man of many parts and accomplishments. From being a Biblical Scholar to a father, husband, author, teaching evangelist, pastor, and Gospel team leader, he has experienced a wide range of roles in his lifetime. Born and raised in Nigeria, he grew up in a Christian home and was exposed to Christian teachings from an early age. His parents were both devoted Christians, and this had a significant impact on his life.

He attended the Prestigious Yaba College of Technology, Nigeria, where he was studying Electrical Engineering before he was called into the ministry. After much struggle with his maker, he realized that his true calling was to become a servant of the Lord. He then yielded to the call and studied Theology both at the Baptist College of Theology, Oyo, and the Prestigious Nigerian Baptist Theological Seminary, Ogbomoso, Oyo State, Nigeria, where he earned a Diploma in Theology (2002), Bachelor of Theology (Missiology) and Bachelors of Arts at the University of Ibadan (2008). His quest for knowledge led him to further his studies at the Postgraduate level both at the University of Ibadan and the ECWA Theological Seminary, Igbaja where he bagged both a Master of Arts in New Testament Studies (2012) and a Doctor of Ministry in Pulpit Ministry (2017).

John Olukunle Odejayi is the team leader of "the Gospel Heralds", a Christian gospel organization that is dedicated to sharing the gospel around the world. One of his biggest passions is writing books. He has authored some books, including "Where is My Spouse?', Jesus' Healings and the Miraculous, Flee and Follow, and lots more."

John Olukunle Odejayi is a devoted family man. He is married to Ruth Adeola Odejayi, a fellow minister of the gospel and Christian educator and they have three daughters together. He believes that family is a crucial aspect of life and fulfilling ministry, and he actively supports his wife and daughters in their endeavors.

John Olukunle Odejayi is a man who has dedicated his life to serving God and spreading his word. From being a pastor to an author, teaching evangelist, and family man, his story is inspiring. He has touched the lives of many people through his ministry work, and his contributions to Christian studies have been significant. He is proof that when we dedicate our lives to something that speaks to our hearts, we can make a real difference in the world.

www.ingramcontent.com/pod-product-compliance
Lightning Source LLC
Chambersburg PA
CBHW051845250726
48659CB00006B/2038